DIGITAL LEARNING STRATEGIES

How do I assign and assess 21st century work?

Michael **FISHER**

 Alexandria, VA USA

ASCD | arias™

Website: www.ascd.org   www.ascdarias.org
E-mail: books@ascd.org

Printed in the United States of America. Cover art © 2013 by ASCD. ASCD publications present a variety of viewpoints. The views expressed or implied in this book should not be interpreted as official positions of the Association.

PAPERBACK ISBN: 978-1-4166-1864-5   ASCD product #SF114045

Also available as an e-book (see Books in Print for the ISBNs).

Library of Congress Cataloging-in-Publication Data for this title was delayed due to the government shutdown of fall 2013. CIP data will be available in MARC records or at http://catalog.loc.gov/.

21 20 19 18 17 16 15 14 13   1 2 3 4 5 6 7 8 9 10

DIGITAL LEARNING STRATEGIES

How do I assign and assess 21st century work?

Want to earn a free ASCD Arias e-book?
Your opinion counts! Please take 2–3 minutes to give
us your feedback on this publication. All survey
respondents will be entered into a drawing to
win an ASCD Arias e-book.

Please visit
www.ascd.org/ariasfeedback

Thank you!

Introduction

In the 21st century, we enjoy a lot of conveniences that would have been inconceivable a hundred years ago—the World Wide Web, video conferencing, mobile devices—yet so much of how we teach students remains stubbornly traditional. Is this because, as Heidi Hayes Jacobs (2010) quips, we enjoy preparing kids for 1973? Is it because we're scared that robots will someday replace teachers? Is the proliferation of information and technology just too overwhelming for us to consider better and more convenient ways of doing things? Whatever the reason, it's just not okay anymore to ignore the changing faces of our students and of the tools that we use to educate them.

So what do we do now? I believe it boils down to two words: *Think immersive.* I want technology to be what water is to a fish; what air is to a human; what the Force is to Luke Skywalker. *Immersed in technology* is what classrooms in the 21st century must be, with digital tools an always-available choice rather than a planned-for event.

"Mental Velcro"

In her book *Active Literacy Across the Curriculum*, Heidi Hayes Jacobs discusses the creation of instructional activities that activate what she calls "mental Velcro" for students, writing that "students need to know the 'sticking point' when they engage in reading, listening, and viewing" (Jacobs, 2006, p. 45).

One of my mentors—Vivian Demers-Jagoda, a teacher and brain-based learning specialist—used to discuss with me the importance of mental Velcro for students. To illustrate, she once asked me to share what I remembered about 7th grade. I listed some memories: attending a big school dance, entering an art contest, dissecting frogs in science class. Vivian asked me how often I had done these things. I answered that they'd happened only once—in the 7th grade. Then she asked me to try to remember three worksheets I had completed that year, or a question from a math test, or even a topic from my Social Studies textbook. I couldn't do it.

The moral here? *"Different" matters.* Anything we do that's different from the norm creates mental Velcro. Digital tools provide us with these opportunities.

Strategic Choices

In the United States, the Common Core State Standards for English Language Arts paint a picture of modern students who do the following:

- Work independently.
- Value content knowledge.
- Are attentive to new tasks, purposes, disciplines, and audiences (many of the latter with a global perspective).
- Think critically and value evidence when drawing conclusions and making decisions.
- Use the Internet and digital media strategically and capably (National Governor's Association, 2010).

As the last item in the above list suggests, digital tools bring with them entirely new menus of options suitable for a variety of classroom purposes that students can potentially use strategically and capably. Consider book reports, for example: The traditional five-to-seven-paragraph summary of a book can now be a series of blog posts, a book trailer, or an interactive slideshow. We've come a long way, though we still have a long way to go for these menus of options to be the norm for every student in every school.

The Tools of Today
to Prepare for Tomorrow

My grandfather recently gave my brother and me some tools that had belonged to my great-grandfather, Alonzo McDaniel, who was equal parts farmer and carpenter. One of these is an early 20th century drill—the type with a drive wheel and a turning handle with a screw-in chuck. I would be unlikely to actually use this tool, as my electric drill is much more efficient.

The same could be said of the tools used in the traditional classroom: The majority of tasks for which they're used haven't changed, but the efficiency and effectiveness with which those tasks can be accomplished has improved greatly thanks to new technology. In order to create mental Velcro and achieve digital immersion, we need to consider what devices and applications need to be as ubiquitous as pencils in the modern classroom.

In Ryan Graham's 8th grade math classes at Kannapolis Middle School in North Carolina, students are surrounded by technology with which they can demonstrate their learning from day one. Mr. Graham knows that in order to increase proficiency students need to not only be able to solve complex problems, but also to articulate the steps necessary to get to a solution. He lets students select and use interactive digital tools for this purpose. Although he doesn't spend a whole lot of time teaching the use of any one tool, he does introduce new tools to his students regularly— sometimes in the form of a minilesson about the tool, other times by casually mentioning it as something that students might want to discover on their own. One such tool is Prezi, a virtual whiteboard for creating online presentations: Mr. Graham told his students about it and shared the URL, then left it up to them to investigate and determine whether it would be a good tool for them to have in their toolboxes.

One of Mr. Graham's students, Caroline, used Prezi to create a presentation on solving multistep equations (accessible here: prezi.com/ctc91_2ct5jq/untitled-prezi/). This digital tool allowed her to demonstrate her learning by showing her work and using text to explain the steps. By allowing Caroline the freedom to show her learning using a tool of her choice, Mr. Graham helped her to take greater ownership of her work; and by letting Caroline add visuals and animation to her presentation, Prezi offered her an opportunity to create mental Velcro, thus helping to attach the learning in her brain. In the end, Caroline created a product of value that now lives online for others to see—her peers, perhaps, or perhaps even students learning multistep equations somewhere across the globe.

Toolboxes and Solution Fluency

I'm reminded often of the tools that are in my physical toolbox at home, including the new (old) ones from my great-grandfather. All of them where designed for specific purposes—and yet, because I have them in my toolbox, I am free to think of innovative ways to combine them or use them for purposes beyond those for which they were originally designed. This is precisely what we want students to be able to do with the tools in their toolboxes.

It would be very easy for me to list here the essential digital tools that every student should know how to use. However, such a list could be interpreted as advocating tool-specific planning, which I do not. Instead, I'll direct you toward the collection of tools, tutorials, and classroom examples that I've set up on the following webpage: www. livebinders.com/play/play?id=1021963.

The bigger point I want to make has to do with solution fluency—that is, "fluency with regard to solving a problem using the toolboxes and resources a student has collected over the course of his or her academic career" (Fisher & Tribuzzi, in press). Students need a variety of experiences with multiple tools so that they can add them to their digital toolboxes, and they need to know what tools to choose for particular tasks.

A word of caution: though tools can be of great use to students, they can also have drawbacks. Sometimes they are so new and exciting that they only attract students on a surface level. No matter the tools being used, teachers must ensure that students are working rigorously, listening to feedback, and revising their work accordingly. The tools should never overshadow the intended task or learning objective.

Assigning Digital Work

From conducting simple vocabulary practice online to leveraging multiple platforms for complex demonstrations of learning, digital tools can be used for 21st century work in many ways in our classrooms.

I propose asking the following six questions when considering whether digital work is suitable for a classroom task:

1. What is the learning objective? When making decisions about whether to include digital tools in a lesson, the learning objective needs to always remain the focus. As Perry Marshall (2013) once put it, "No one who ever bought a drill wanted a drill, they wanted a hole." The task at hand must meet the parameters of the learning objective while also offering students a choice of ways in which to demonstrate their learning.

2. Is the task worthy of a digital upgrade? Or is this just a worksheet on an iPad? Simply automating is not what we want —that's just bolting technology onto an already-in-place practice (November, 2010). Digital work is about *interaction and creation*, not simply access and consumption. We want students to think about the resources available to them and use them in ways that are new and exciting—ways that create mental Velcro.

3. Will digital tools increase or decrease the cognitive rigor of the task? According to Norman Webb's Depths of Knowledge theory, there are four main levels of interacting with content. In ascending order of cognitive rigor, these levels are *recall, application, strategic thinking,* and *extended thinking* (Hess, 2006). If digital tools encourage no greater rigor than that expected for the level of recall, then they may not be worth using. Digital tools should invite students toward higher levels of rigor.

4. Does the digital upgrade involve collaboration, communication, creative problem solving, or creative thinking? Digital tools are only as good as (and peripheral to) the 21st century skills that they engage: collaboration, communication, creative problem solving, and creative thinking. Students will need time to collaboratively explore and reflect upon the decisions they make.

5. Are sufficient digital tools available and do all students have access to them? Consider what tools are available for students to use at school if they don't have them at home. Are the resources equitable for all students?

6. Are the students involved in some of the decision making? We teach at an awesome time when students often know as much or more than teachers about digital tools. Inviting students to share their opinions as to what tools they'd prefer to use helps to foster their engagement and activate mental Velcro.

Here's an example of effectively using technology in class after careful consideration of the above six questions. In 2011, I visited Stephen Wilmarth's classroom at the Number 1 Middle School affiliated to Central China Normal University in Wuhan, China—the first classroom in that country to start a one-iPad-per-student initiative. Mr. Wilmarth used iPads to greatly modernize instruction, effectively eliminating the need for the stacks of cumbersome materials known to bow students' desks. One way that students used these devices was to practice their English language fluency using word-game apps such as Bookworm and Words with Friends—apps that the students themselves had suggested at Mr. Wilmarth's invitation. The games helped students meet their learning objective of increased fluency in a way that's more engaging than traditional modes of practice—and because students almost always played the games together, their use of technology was collaborative.

Here is how we might apply our six key questions to the example of iPad word-fluency apps:

1. What is the learning objective? The learning objective is increased fluency, beginning with high-frequency words and moving eventually to more academic-level words. The games on the iPad help students meet this learning objective in a fun and effective way; some of them even give students additional information about the words, such as contextual examples.

2. Is the task worthy of a digital upgrade? I'm sure that if you asked the students, they'd say that the apps are more engaging than traditional modes of fluency practice (e.g., writing words over and over, memorizing lists upon lists of them).

3. Will digital tools increase or decrease the cognitive rigor of the task? The answer here would depend on the original version of the task. If it simply asked students to recall information, then the apps do increase the rigor somewhat, because students are required to learn how to play and complete the games.

4. Does the digital upgrade involve collaboration, communication, creative problem solving, or creative thinking? Collaboration and communication are definitely involved here, as students almost always play the games together, even though they each have their own iPad. They would often search for words together or make decisions about correct spelling or what words might mean.

5. Are sufficient digital tools available and do all students have access to them? The answer is yes—every student has an iPad and the same access to apps.

6. Are the students involved in some of the decision making? Students are allowed to suggest potentially useful games and choose the ones that they will ultimately play.

From Novelty to Sophistication

Based on my own observations, digital tools are too often little more than novelty products that don't extend students' knowledge or allow them to demonstrate high levels of learning. Many digital tools allow kids to do things that are fun and engaging but that don't truly tap into their creativity and critical thinking. It's not necessarily a bad thing to start at the novelty level with digital tools, if only to get a feel for them, but digital instruction should become increasingly sophisticated.

Here's an example. At Meriwether Lewis Elementary School in Charlottesville, Virginia, 3rd grade teacher Michael Thornton begins a lesson by discussing with his students the following standard from the state of Virginia: "The student will investigate and understand basic patterns and cycles occurring in nature. Key concepts include patterns of natural events such as day and night, seasonal changes, simple phases of the moon, and tides; animal life cycles; and plant life cycles" (Virginia Department of Education, 2010).

After discussing what the standard means with his students, Mr. Thornton lets them find their own relevant online resources and share them through a collaborative Google document that Mr. Thornton creates and all students can access. Along with adding resources related to the standard to the document, the students include explanations of how useful and applicable each resource is to their work.

Once students have selected a fair number of online resources and added them to the Google document, they whittle the list down to a few key choices and embed their contents to a LiveBinders page. (You can access Mr. Thornton's LiveBinders page here: http://www.livebinders.com/play/play?id=61256#.) The students then create their own quizzes using Google's Forms app, which they add to a separate LiveBinders page. Students read the articles and take the quizzes that their peers create. Mr. Thornton also posts links to the LiveBinders pages on Twitter and Facebook, asking his entire social network to take the quizzes as well. Any answers to the quiz questions are automatically collected in a Google spreadsheet and reviewed by Mr. Thornton and his students. This is a great opportunity not only for Mr. Thornton to informally assess his students, but also for him to address any misconceptions that the range of answers suggests.

It would be fairly easy for students simply to find resources online, list them on a LiveBinders page, and leave it at that. But what does this demonstrate about learning? It's a novelty-level use of technology. For this to be a good assignment, we're looking, even at a 3rd grade level, for more sophisticated actions from students, such as justifying the inclusion of their chosen resources. Finding the resources only addresses the investigation portion of the standard; students need to demonstrate understanding as well. Through the Google quizzes, Mr. Thornton is finding out what students are learning and retaining. And because students have to articulate the reasoning behind their choice of resources, Mr. Thornton has given them the gift of discernment—a critical-thinking skill tied deeply to understanding.

Digital Citizenship and Information Literacy

When assigning digital work, it's important to teach students about appropriate online behaviors—for example, how to provide constructive feedback, attribute shared work, and cite references. Such behaviors can be introduced through minilessons focused on creating and analyzing digital content.

I often hear from teachers who are upset that their students misuse technology by copying and pasting from online sources and calling the work their own. Yet I have seen some of these same teachers deliver presentations that clearly include content and images found online and used without attribution or permission. If we are to hold our students accountable for proper digital etiquette, we as teachers must model appropriate behavior.

Assessing Digital Work

Digital work can be used for both formative and summative assessment. Students can be assessed either inside or out of the classroom, depending on the digital tools being used: Some tools—such as Socrative, Poll Everywhere, and Text the Mob—are specifically designed to let teachers quickly collect multiple types of information, including survey results, objective and subjective student answers, and in-the-moment data that could shift the teaching and learning experience on a dime.

Not all digital work needs to be formally assessed. Think back to Mr. Wilmarth's students and their fluency practice on their iPads: Mr. Wilmarth will be able to make suggestions during fluency practice that will guide students to better learning, but he is not grading them. That said, assessment is meant to demonstrate student learning, not the mere completion of a task; it's *you know, you show, you go*, not *you do, you check off, you continue*.

When assessing digital work, consider the following four primary factors:

1. Students should demonstrate learning. Regardless of the digital tools used, the final product should demonstrate that students are learning what you intend for them to learn and have met the rigors of both the assignment and relevant standards. The assessment shouldn't tell us more about the tool than about the student's work using the tool.

2. Students should demonstrate content proficiency. Students should demonstrate proficiency at their grade level in a particular content area. The work that they do should reflect high degrees of understanding, application, analysis, and evaluation of content and associated skills.

3. Students should reflect upon and articulate why they've selected a particular digital tool, what they learned, and how audience interaction affected the resulting product. Students need to be able to reflect on and discuss why they did what they did and how the end result represents both their learning and the trial-and-error nature of problem solving and discovery.

4. Students should give credit where credit is due for sources found online. They need to be taught what they can and cannot borrow, what Creative Commons licensing means, and how to search for and use appropriate content.

Rubrics

Rubrics can be used to assess the primary factors noted above as well as such other factors as vocabulary usage, depth of learning, thoughtful input into other's revisions, and reflections. In their book *Teaching and Assessing 21st Century Skills* (2011), Marzano and Heflebower propose a five-value scale for developing assessment tools that ranges from zero (for lack of success despite assistance) to four (for achieving complex learning goals). Similarly, in a wiki devoted to different types of rubrics (http://qualityrubrics. pbworks.com/), Learner Centered Initiatives proposes task-specific rubrics, with levels ranging from *novice* to *mentor*, that include language particular to the task at hand (Borgioli, 2011). These types of rubrics are the most relevant for assessing digital work.

Although rubrics can be used in a variety of ways, I personally think it's important that they give students opportunities both to see what quality looks like and to improve their work, so that they can understand that their learning is valued over the end product. When creating a rubric, teachers should model 21st century skills such as communication and collaboration by clearly describing the rubric's levels and the differences among them as well as the specific content knowledge that the rubric is designed to assess.

On her website, blogging teacher Silvia Rosenthal Tolisano shows how to use rubrics to determine the quality of students' blog posts and includes several examples. You can access the post here: http://langwitches.org/blog/2011/12/25/learning-about-blogs-for-your-students-part-vii-quality/. She created her rubrics with input from virtual colleagues to allow students to understand what "quality" looks like at varying levels of proficiency.

The following online resources offer examples of rubrics suitable for assessing digital work and advice for creating them:

- The University of Wisconsin's collection of rubrics designed to assess digital work: http://www.uwstout.edu/soe/profdev/rubrics.cfm
- Ryan Bretag's Creative Commons–licensed rubric for assessing student blogs: https://docs.google.com/document/d/1z7FU72kQvvzUHxP5664SOXdVn5z-p7D4i5wc1WJSaOM/preview
- Richard Byrne's blog post, "5 Ways to Blow the Top Off of Rubrics": http://www.freetech4teachers.com/2013/04/5-ways-to-blow-top-off-of-rubrics.html
- DigiTales' scoring guides for evaluating digital projects: http://digitales.us/evaluating-projects/scoring-guides
- EdTechTeacher's extensive collection of guidelines and resources: http://edtechteacher.org/index.php/teaching-technology/assessment-rubrics

- Cybraryman's catalog of resources related to rubrics: http://www.cybraryman.com/rubrics.html

Digital Portfolios

Digital portfolios are a great way for students to demonstrate both what they've learned and how they learned it. Portfolios can consist of anything from entries in a student-created blog to a compendium of online products housed on a website such as LiveBinders or EduClipper—the possibilities are endless!

Most digital portfolios include a reflective statement by the student. You might ask your students to reflect on why they chose to use a particular digital tool for the portfolio, what considerations they had to work through in order to create a quality product, how they invited global feedback on the drafts within the portfolio, and how they used the feedback to create their final product.

You can access a list of resources related to digital portfolios that I created here: http://www.livebinders.com/play/play?id=647327. Of particular interest is a link to an interview that my friend and colleague, Allison Zmuda, conducted with another of our colleagues, David Niguidula—a pioneering expert on the use of digital portfolios in the classroom. Niguidula explains that with digital portfolios, "students are collecting and reflecting on work that they're going to show to somebody else" (Zmuda, 2012). The key word in that quote is *reflecting*: Digital portfolios allow students to demonstrate what they've learned by showing the process of learning rather than just a final product. Niguidula further notes that digital portfolios "can do two things: allow a student to demonstrate standards, and show who the student is as an individual learner. Students are showing that they are meeting the standards—but each student is showing his or her own personal approach and aspirations" (Zmuda, 2012).

In my experience, two specific types of portfolios allow for especially strong demonstrations of student learning: digital presentation portfolios and digital process portfolios. In digital presentation portfolios, students select what they believe to be their best digital work. Each piece is accompanied by a reflective commentary on the reasons for including it, preferably along with an overall reflection on how the portfolio demonstrates the student's process of learning. By contrast, digital process portfolios document learning over the duration of a given assignment. For example, in the case of a research project, a digital process portfolio might include such items as statements and claims, lists of resources both considered and chosen (with reflective commentary on why the chosen ones were picked), outlines, drafts, revisions, and the final version of the project.

Online Feedback

Ideally, items intended for digital portfolios would be posted somewhere online to solicit feedback from a diverse audience (teachers, classmates, local and international peers) that could help focus revisions. Students can create, share, and comment on content in a variety of ways online. One such way is through Storybird, an online platform that allows students to share and revise digital work. "Cal's Story About

Knight" (http://storybird.com/books/calebs-story-about-knight/) is a great example. This story was written by Cal, an awesome 2nd grader I worked with in North Carolina. When trying to demonstrate the virtues of Storybird to an audience of skeptical teachers, I invited Cal to help show how the site worked. Although he'd never used Storybird before, he was able to use it with only some basic directions. In 10 minutes or so, he completed this draft of his story.

After Cal left the class, the assembled teachers and I took a look at his work. For a 2nd grader who had never used Storybird before, his effort wasn't bad. The tool allowed us to examine specific issues that he needed help with: how to tell a cohesive story from beginning to end, for example, and certain issues of grammar and punctuation. One anonymous commenter on his work noted the he replaced "are" for "is" in one of his sentences. How powerful is that? Global observations lead to revision.

I specifically asked Cal not to revise "Cal's Story About Knight," as I like being able to share it with other educators. In other pieces that Cal has written since, both his teacher and members of the global Storybird community have contributed to his becoming a better writer. Such online formative assessments allow Cal's teachers to target his individual needs and address them immediately.

Amplified Revising

By working online, Cal is engaged in *amplified revising*—that is, shifting the potential audience for a student's work. Amplified revising gives students opportunities for improvement that they've never had before by activating a global cadre of audience members and soliciting feedback from them. I would love to see teachers assess students based not only on their demonstrations of learning, but also on the amount of online feedback they've solicited when preparing to revise their work.

Almost all of the new digital tools that students can use to demonstrate their learning allow the audience to provide feedback for the author, whether it's as involved as articulating reactions to the work via comments (quality feedback) or as simple as clicking "like" on a post (not quality feedback).

In modern classrooms, the teacher cannot remain the only audience for whom students prepare. Amplified revising gives students new perspectives and divergent thinking opportunities that make their work more relevant, more real, and more awesome than ever before.

More Examples of Digital Work

The following two examples of digital work exhibit immersion, sophistication, and student-centered instruction.

The JoyceWays app

Professor Joe Nugent of Boston College has taken digital work to the next level with the JoyceWays app. There's a lot to be proud of with this student-created app that offers a ton of information in a James Joyce–inspired guide to Dublin, Ireland.

When creating the app, students had to make decisions about what information to share—specific locations, book excerpts, photos, commentary, and so on. They also had to use technology to generate maps, conduct research, and collect resources. (You can read a blog post about the app here: http://www.bc.edu/content/bc/offices/pubaf/news/2012-jun-aug/joyceways-app.html.) Though many students contributed to the project, one core group did much of the work, including traveling, photographing, fundraising, and marketing. Since its creation, the app has been featured in the *Washington Post*, the *Los Angeles Times*, the Huffington Post, ABC News, and more.

I think it's obvious that the JoyceWays app represents a very sophisticated use of digital tools: The students created a product of value that is nationally recognized and that people are paying to use, and they had to familiarize themselves deeply with James Joyce's work to do something that they'd never been able to do before.

The JoyceWays app represents a demonstration of learning far and above the other examples included here—partly because it involves students at the college level, and partly because it was a multiyear project assigned by a creative, risk-taking professor whose students were willing to be challenged at a high level. Clearly, the goal of the assignment is to represent Joyce's Dublin, not simply to create an app.

There's a reflective component to the JoyceWays project in the form of an appeal for funds on the website Kickstarter, which allows users to raise money for projects (a process known as "crowdfunding"). The students used Kickstarter to explain the goal of their project, the work they'd done so far, and what they intended to do with the app when it was completed.

The JoyceWays app is available through the iTunes App store, where it is open to ratings and reviews. For the most part, these have been favorable and offered comments that go beyond opinionated niceties. One of the comments even suggested that the app is somewhat sloppily edited—something for the creators to consider when updating it.

Though the creators of the JoyceWays app are in college, digital tools give us the ability to create similar assignments for students at all grade levels and in all content areas.

Multiyear Marketing Project

One of the most exciting projects I've worked on in the last few years is a still-ongoing, multiyear e-book project that began as a potential fundraiser for the Martin J. Gottlieb Day School in Jacksonville, Florida. Students were provided with poems that I had written over a decade ago and given the challenge of creating an illustrated e-book out of them. (I served as the students' "virtual coach" for the project.) Over time, the project has come to include the process of marketing the e-books. As the project has progressed, students have demonstrated learning related to writing conventions, persuasive and informational writing, vocabulary acquisition, and even statistical scenarios for predicting how much profit the book might eventually generate.

Students have collaborated on all phases of the project, discussing their illustration ideas and soliciting feedback from each other, their teachers, and me through email and Skype. A blog post by one of their teachers, Silvia Rosenthal Tolisano, discusses the types of interactions the students have had and how they've articulated the next steps of the project. (You can read the post here: http://langwitches.org/blog/2013/05/03/entrepreneurialism-student-voices-and-authentic-work/.) Because the teachers and the students have blogged about their experiences, they've also garnered quite a bit of feedback from a global audience about their work.

The students are laser-focused on their task: to market their collaborative work as a fundraiser for their school while engaging in multiple roles to learn a vast array of skills that aren't in any of their textbooks. Students will spend the next school year publishing an e-book, creating a marketing campaign, and considering their target demographics. As a matter of fact, as I was sitting here writing this paragraph, I received an e-mail from some of the students inviting me to view a spreadsheet on which they'd collaborated, and the students opened up a chat using the TodaysMeet program to discuss the project.

On a Saturday. Outside of school. On their own time.

As a teacher or coach, virtual or otherwise, this is the equivalent of winning the teaching lottery. Thinking and choices matter. These kids are creating powerful mental Velcro.

Digital Learning Libraries

One exciting aspect of digital products is the opportunity that they provide for schools to build repositories of student-created content that both represent the collective learning of students and allow students to continue to teach each other and build rigor as they progress through school. The material housed in these digital libraries can function as "set points" from which students can create more rigorous and complex products.

In our book *Upgrade Your Curriculum*, Janet Hale and I include a matrix for considering the best use of digital-video learning libraries. We note that students should "self-plan their task, their purpose, and their potential audience to create videos for learning in student- or team-selected" tools (Hale & Fisher, 2013, p. 162). Students can categorize the videos and perhaps think about grouping them using a web tool that allows for comments and feedback. YouTube, for example, allows users to create channels for a class, school, or district; has multiple options for interacting via comments or social media; and even has editing tools that students can use to revise their work based on feedback.

Digital learning libraries don't need to be devoted to videos: Students could potentially create libraries of multiple types of digital products categorized by content or grade level. When students create embeddable digital products of any kind, they create mental Velcro for themselves while simultaneously creating authentic study resources for their peers. Think of how great it would be for schools to have their own Khan Academy–like collections created by their own students! As time goes by and more digital content is created, students can sort it into searchable databases and tag each item by content area, digital-tool type, grade level, and so on. Think about the effect such a database—a virtual museum of student learning on multiple grade levels!—could have on future student work and instructional planning from year to year.

If your school doesn't have a website (which it should), or if your website doesn't have the capabilities to house a digital library (in which case, upgrade it), you can save student work online. In the case of digital videos, you can create a channel on YouTube where you can upload videos and tag them with different key words. LiveBinders and EduClipper go further, allowing you to embed different types of digital content in addition to videos. All three sites allow for feedback in comments sections.

By creating digital work and organizing it in digital libraries, students are innovating in ways that weren't even possible until very recently. Bodies of work that used to encompass cumbersome file folders filled with physical student work are now weightless and easily searchable, allowing us to reflect on our students' learning from the moment their digital footprints are created.

Students as Educational Partners

We live in a world where teachers, though still extremely important, don't exert the same influence that they used to. Students don't need teachers to gift them with knowledge anymore, because knowledge and content are all around them. What students really need is help deciphering, exploring, and curating all of that information; teachers help students make these connections. Students need opportunities to feel as though they are in educational partnerships with teachers—a zone of mutual respect, proficiency, and wisdom.

Charlotte Danielson's widely used rubrics for improving teacher practice include a subdomain for designing student assessments in which she shares that distinguished teachers' plans "contain evidence of student contribution to [the assessments'] development" (2009, p. 331). She also notes that assessments should be evaluated partly on whether they "provide opportunities for student choice" and allow students to "participate in designing assessments for their own work" (p. 332). Students who are given choices as to both how they approach assignments and how their work is assessed are being given opportunities for engagement, for strategic thinking, and for deeper learning. If teachers want to have a huge impact on student learning and engagement, then they need to focus on "student-centered ownership of learning. Students not only create content and choose software and web-based tools to use, but also make choices based on specific tasks, purposes, and audiences" (Hale & Fisher, 2013, p. 22). The identity of the teacher in the modern classroom is shifting from *sage on the stage* to *guide on the side*—that is, from rote delivery of content to coaching and facilitating problem solving.

Conclusion

So there you have it. What have you read here that will affect your professional practice around assigning and assessing digital work? What is the next step in your action plan for putting what you've learned into practice? Will you elect to improve your own digital toolbox so that you can share the tools with your own students? Will you analyze some of your instructional tasks to see if a digital upgrade might be worthwhile? Will you analyze digital assignments and look for ways to increase their rigor and sophistication? Will you create rubrics or perhaps consider using digital portfolios to assess student learning?

If you're not sure what your next steps should be, I'd like to reemphasize a little advice:

Think immersive.

Think about your students and the world in which they live. Think about whether or not the work they are doing in your classroom is preparing them for higher education or a 21st century career. Think about how your students want to demonstrate their learning. Think about how digital devices and applications are the new pencils and paper. If these tools are always available, how does that change the way we educate our students?

Think immersive.

To give your feedback on this publication
and be entered into a drawing for a
free ASCD Arias e-book, please visit
www.ascd.org/ariasfeedback

ASCD | arias™

ENCORE

10 INSTRUCTIONAL BRAINSTORMS

When I work with schools and teachers, I often have opportunities to brainstorm ways to invigorate instruction with digital assignments and assessments. Following are some potential brainstorms based on already-in-practice instructional strategies that could serve as new digital forms of schoolwork. All of the ideas included here came from actual curriculum maps from schools around the country; they represent both content pieces and new ways of engaging in more traditional instructional practices. (Although many of them point to web resources rather than to device-specific applications, most of the web resources either have companion apps or can be accessed on a variety of digital devices.)

This is an excellent time for you to collaborate with your content-area and grade-level peers to find new ways of exploring the potential of digital tools. Modern work is a difficult endeavor to embark on alone. Having multiple voices and experiences at the planning table creates better opportunities for better instruction than a single person could ever devise.

Perhaps I should adjust the motto: *Think immersive— and work together.*

◯ **1. Reader's Response Journals.** When students participate in minilessons around writing strategies and processes, they are often expected to document, in writing, how they can apply those strategies in their work. There are multiple ways to digitize this process. For example, students might blog about the strategies, which opens up opportunities for a wider audience and amplified revisions. Students can also use collaborative tools like Google Drive, where they can invite select users to offer commentary and advice for revisions focused on specific topics (e.g., grammar, flow, focus, attribution of sources).

⬤ **2. Cell Projects.** In middle school science, students are often tasked with identifying and explaining cell structures. Though the standards often include the words *identify* and *explain*, they don't specify *how* students are expected to do complete these tasks. In many schools, students demonstrate that they can identify and explain cell parts by conducting a "cell project" that may consist of printed pictures, written explanations, models, tri-fold boards, and so on.

When a cell project is digitized, it becomes a more complex task: Deeper thinking is required when students must go beyond identifying and explaining to also evaluate, navigate, and create a digital product. Students might consider using wikis (e.g., Wikispaces, PBWiki) or website creation tools (e.g., Weebly, WordPress) to create online cell projects. Students can document both lower level thinking (e.g., by identifying the parts of a cell) and higher level thinking (e.g., by creating visualizations or documenting experiments that they created to observe the parts of a cell and how they function).

◯ **3. Textbook Alternatives.** Reading a textbook is still the *modus operandi* in many classrooms. Students still need access to information contained in the text, but because that information can now be found everywhere, the text becomes just one more resource for students to use. If in the past the textbook was the anchor of instruction, now it's one of many paving stones on the path to comprehension and learning.

In the modern classroom, digital reading tasks have a different set of associated skills than traditional texts. With traditional texts, students need to know how to identify a text's structure and organization; with digital texts, students need to also know how to navigate the material. For example, they may need to engage with interactive elements such as maps or figures, look up definitions to words in the moment, or follow hyperlinks to explore related material before returning to continue navigating the text. Clearly, this process goes beyond simply reading the text. In the 21st century, text is experienced on multiple levels and through multiple types of media, requiring deeper attention and focus than traditional text.

◯ **4. Research Papers.** I would like to believe that college and career readiness demand that teachers teach their students multiple ways to demonstrate what they've learned through research. Digital alternatives to research papers should be task-focused but not tradition-driven: Students must still be able to either make a claim and provide evidence for it or to write informatively about a topic, but they can represent their learning in any number of modern ways. For instance, there are many online tools, such as Smore and Piktochart, that allow students to make infographics. (Not sure what those are? Do a Google image search for "infographic" and have a gander at the awesomeness that appears.) For more quantitative research, students might consider using Google Forms or Survey Monkey, which allows them to design a survey and distribute it online via email, Facebook, Twitter, or any other digital means. They can then use the information gleaned from the survey either in a traditional research paper, an infographic, or in a digital presentation using any number of online tools.

⭕ **5. Interactive Posters.** When working on a unit on early civilizations, I noticed that my fellow teachers were expecting their students to differentiate between different types of early hominids both orally and in writing. I wondered how online poster-creation tools like Glogster or Thinglink might help teachers to upgrade this task. Students could locate drawings or images related to their hominid type, then add features such as videos, text, additional images, voice overs, and so on to make their posters interactive. Teachers could host the students' posters on their own websites so that classmates could access each other's posters, which in turn would allow them to write comparative analyses of all the different types of hominids.

⚪ **6. Text Annotation.** In the past, teachers might have asked their students to annotate text by writing notes in the margins or placing sticky notes on the text. Today, there are many web tools (e.g., Padlet, NoteApp) and apps (e.g., Infinote, Corkulous) that students can use for digital annotations. (If you'd like to investigate the topic of "annotexting" further, check out the ASCD blog post I wrote with my colleague Jeanne Tribuzzi here: http://edge. ascd.org/_ANNOTEXTING/blog/5820097/127586.html.)

⚪ **7. Reenactments and Dramatic Representations.** I've worked with many teachers over the years who do reenactments or dramatic representations of the content that they teach. This act of going beyond the text is great for creating mental Velcro—and it can also be done digitally! There are some really cool tools online such as xTraNormal and Wideo that allow students to easily make animated movies. The only real skill required of students for these is that of writing dialogue; the rest is just a matter of learning to interact with characters, elements, settings, backgrounds, and so on. This type of assignment enhances content-area literacy as well!

⚪ **8. Notetaking.** Notetaking is still something that millions of students are doing daily in classrooms around the world, and it too can be digitized. Individual students can use writing apps on their digital devices or software on their computers to save digital versions of notes that they can then easily modify and share via email. For collaborative notetaking, apps and tools such as Google Docs, Draftin, Qikpad , and Today's Meet allow students to crowdsource notetaking so that everyone contributes notes, associated media, and hyperlinks in real time. Students could even take notes by devising a special hashtag to use on Twitter, then searching for that hashtag to find more information from a potentially large and global audience.

⭕ **9. Comparative Analysis of Current Events.** In March of 2011, the world watched in horror as one of the most powerful earthquakes ever recorded hit Japan, followed by an equally powerful tsunami that devastated parts of the country with catastrophic losses of life, shelter, and livelihood. When major news events like this happen, teachers often take them as teachable moments to help students explore news reports and learn about associated issues. There are myriad online resources and apps that allow for digital access to news sources, but a couple of really cool ones have upped the ante for aiding cognition. One of the newest is a website called Newsela, which allows students to explore news stories at different reading levels and take quizzes on the stories that are also differentiated. What's neat about this is that it gives all the students in the classroom an equal footing from which to discuss the news. (I think this counts as "digital differentiation"!)

When working in schools around the time of the Japanese earthquake, I showed teachers how to use the website Wordle to create tag clouds of different news stories. This enabled them to conduct out-of-context comparative analyses to see what aspects of the catastrophe (e.g., the science of the earthquake, human interest stories) were emphasized by different news agencies. I also showed them how to use a service called Newspapermap to compare news stories from the United States with those from around the world. This particular web tool also houses news stories from as far back as a century ago. It lets you sort newspapers by language and even translates foreign newspapers into English. This is a website that kicks learning up 10 notches by allowing for a global investigation into what was happening around the world on a particular day: For example, I found it fascinating to discover what domestic newspapers were reporting around September 6, 1901, the day President McKinley was shot at the Pan-American Exposition in Buffalo, New York. It took days for the reports to reach the West Coast newspapers, and other countries around the world had different news priorities.

◯ **10. Minecraft.** Students around the world are engaging in the online game Minecraft, which invites players to build three-dimensional structures and materials out of the raw materials of its virtual worlds. There is much to explore here, both in terms of what's already been built into the game and what users can create on their own, and the game's historically accurate worlds offer many opportunities for learning. Minecraft runs on various devices, and there are many user-created tutorials on YouTube that show how to navigate different worlds or build new worlds from scratch. In the game's "creative mode," users are encouraged to build and collaborate and explore with others. (For more information about Minecraft and other opportunities to use gaming in the classroom, search for "gaming" in the clearinghouse at Curriculum21.com.)

Acknowledgments

Gigantic thanks to those who helped me to review and edit: Elizabeth Fisher, Rebecca and Patrick Tharp, Annabelle Howard, and Crista Anderson. You all have eagle eyes and I appreciate your quick feedback!

Much appreciation to Ernesto Yermoli, Genny Ostertag, and Julie Scheina at ASCD. You make my work better with your insights and your amazing ability to condense and add nuance. Thank you.

Major kudos to the following visionary modern-learning educators: Michael Thornton, Stephen Wilmarth, Stephanie Teitelbaum, Shana Gutterman, Ryan Graham, and Joe Nugent. Your modern work with students is exciting and will help many educators with their own professional practice.

Extra-special thanks to Silvia Rosenthal Tolisano, Andrea Hernandez, Janet Hale, and Heidi Hayes Jacobs for being edu-awesome and for being my constant mentors. The incredible work you all do enriches the lives of students around the world.

To the students and staff of the Martin J. Gottlieb Day School in Jacksonville, Florida: I really enjoy all of the awesome time I get to spend with you both virtually and physically, innovating and experimenting. Your students are world-class thinkers and modern day marvels! I am privileged to call you all friends.

References

Borgioli, J. (2011, October 23). *Learner-centered initiatives' quality rubrics.* Accessed at http://qualityrubrics.pbworks.com/

Danielson, C. (2009). *Implementing the framework for teaching in enhancing professional practice.* Alexandria, VA: ASCD.

Fisher, M., & Tribuzzi, J. (in press). Bridging traditional and modern literacy. In H. Jacobs (Ed.), *Leading the new literacies.* Bloomington, IN: Solution Tree.

Fisher, M. (2012, April 30). [Web log message]. Accessed at http://edge.ascd.org/_Strategic-and-Capable/blog/6041787/127586.html

Fisher, M. (2013, February 24). [Web log message]. Accessed at http://www.middleweb.com/6130/math-tools-for-the-common-core/

Hale, J., & Fisher, M. (2013). *Upgrade your curriculum: Practical ways to transform units and engage students.* Alexandria, VA: ASCD.

Heath, C., & Heath, D. (2011). *Switch, how to change things when change is hard.* New York: Crown Business.

Hess, K. (2006). *Exploring cognitive demand in instruction and assessment.* Dover, NH: National Center for Assessment. Accessed at http://www.nciea.org/publication_PDFs/DOK_ApplyingWebb_KH08.pdf

Jacobs, H. H. (2006). *Active literacy across the curriculum: Strategies for reading, writing, speaking, and listening.* Larchmont, NY: Eye on Education, Inc.

Jacobs, H. H. (2010). *Curriculum 21: Essential education for a changing world.* Alexandria, VA: ASCD.

Marzano, R., & Heflebower, T. (2011). *Teaching and assessing 21st century skills: The classroom strategies series.* Denver, CO: Marzano Research Laboratory.

National Governors Association Center for Best Practices & Council of Chief State School Officers. (2010). *Common Core State Standards for English language arts and literacy in history/social studies, science, and technical subjects.* Washington, DC: Authors.

November, A. (2010). *Empowering students with technology* (2nd ed.). Thousand Oaks, CA: Corwin Press.

P21.org. (2011). *Above and beyond: The story of the 4 c's.* Accessed at http://p21.org/tools-and-resources/abovebeyond4cs

Tolisano, S. R. (2011, December 25). [Web log message].
    Retrieved from http://langwitches.org/blog/2011/12/25/
    learning-about-blogs-for-your-students-part-vii-quality/
Virginia Department of Education. (2010). *Science standards of learning
    for Virginia public schools, grade 3.* Accessed at http://www.doe.vir-
    ginia.gov/testing/sol/standards_docs/science/2010/k-6/stds_science3.
    pdf
Zmuda, A. (2012, November 11). [Web log message]. Accessed
    at http://just-startkidsandschools.com/2012/11/11/
    how-digitial-portfolios-document-and-motivate-learning/

Related Resources

At the time of publication, the following ASCD resources were available (ASCD stock numbers appear in parentheses). For up-to-date information about ASCD resources, go to www.ascd.org. You can search the complete archives of Educational Leadership at http://www.ascd.org/el.

ASCD Edge©
Exchange ideas and connect with other educators interested in education technology on the social networking site ASCD Edge at http://ascdedge.ascd.org.

Print Products
Brain-Based Teaching in the Digital Age by Marilee Sprenger (#110018)
Breaking Free from Myths About Teaching and Learning: Innovation as an Engine for Student Success by Allison Zmuda (#109041)
Curriculum 21: Essential Education for a Changing World by Heidi Hayes Jacobs (#109008)
Teaching Every Student in the Digital Age: Universal Design For Learning by Anne Meyer and David H. Rose (#101042)
Transformational Teaching in the Information Age: Making Why and How We Teach Relevant to Students by Thomas R. Rosebrough and Ralph G. Leverett (#110078)

The Technology Fix: The Promise and Reality of Computers in Our Schools by William D. Pflaum (#104002)

Using Technology With Classroom Instruction That Works, 2nd Edition by Howard Pitler, Elizabeth R. Hubbell, and Matt Kuhn (#112012)

ASCD PD Online® Courses

Technology in Schools: A Balanced Perspective (#PD11OC109)

Technology in Schools: Beyond Word Processing (#PD09OC82)

Technology in Schools: Planning Using The LOCATE Model (#PD09OC83)

Technology in Schools: Teaching Better (#PD 09OC84)

For more information: send e-mail to member@ascd.org; call 1-800-933-2723 or 703-578-9600, press 2; send a fax to 703-575-5400; or write to Information Services, ASCD, 1703 N. Beauregard St., Alexandria, VA 22311-1714 USA.

About the Author

Michael Fisher is an instructional coach and educational consultant specializing in the intersection between instructional technology and curriculum design. He works with districts across the country helping teachers and schools maximize available technology, software, and web-based resources while attending to curriculum design, instructional practices, and assessments. He posts frequently to ASCD Edge (edge.ascd.org), the Curriculum 21 blog (www.curriculum21.com/blog), and his own blog (digigogy.blogspot.com). You can contact him via email at digigogy@gmail.com or by visiting his website at www.digigogy.com.

WHAT KEEPS YOU UP AT NIGHT?

ASCD Arias begin with a burning question and then provide the answers you need today—in a convenient format you can read in one sitting and immediately put into practice. Available in both print and digital editions.

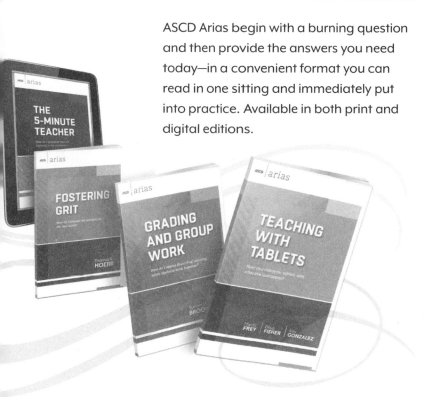

Answers You Need
from Voices You Trust

ASCD | arias™